I0200439

1

Copyright © 2007 john Siwicki/Slabypress. All rights reserved.
No part of this publication may be reproduced, stored in a retrieval
system, or transmitted, in any form or by any means, electronic,
mechanical, photocopying, recording, or otherwise,
without written permission of the author.

ISBN13 978-0-9774118-8-7

For Library of Congress Cataloging-in-Publication Data
please contact publisher

Poetic Art Published by:

SLABYPRESS
W25952 State Road 95
Arcadia, WI 54612
U.S.A.

Order online at:
www.slabypress.com

Technical, Cover, and Book design by JBS

For information contact:
support@slabypress.com

Waldo's warble...

Dream delivers us from dream
and there is no end to the illusion...

...

POEMS

5

POEMS

CHIMBORAZO

Wet, moist, steamy rain water
Falling, rolling onto the leaves
I now hold in my hand
On my port and starboard sides
In front and right behind
Glistening drops of radiant beads
Thunderous as they dive to earth
Sliding and rolling down my face
Over my eyes, across my lips
Down and off my fingertips
Falling in time with the beat
Of millions of other raindrops
A sound rumbles through my soul
Hear and feel drum humming waves
Tickling the bottom of my feet
Taste of heaven on my tongue
I feel each drop rise up through me
Now how can this be done
No mind on earth can conceive
Who knows the secret long kept
That drops through the trees

FLOATING TROPE

Perhaps a figure of speech
Spoken in some non-literal way
Use of a metaphor, who's to say
Interpolated, confusing word or phrase
Embellishment of a story that's told
Songs sung from times that are old
Medieval world people have heard
Liturgies, pieces and plays
Turn around, come back, maze
Roots that have grown deep below
For some time, who can tell
Count the years, begin to yell
Unproductive course, dark blind alley
No hope to lose, against the wall
Last chance, a telephone call
After it's made, part of history
Through a clear lens I see
I have a choice, think wisely
Use the language without regard
This you may come to regret
Into motion the wheels are set
Incongruity, we think it occurs
Asking Santa, while sitting on his knee
I got a rock, the irony
A fisherman tells a tale
Extravagant gross exaggeration
Hyperbole from father to sun

Metaphoric name we supply
Old English, Norse singing
Conventional but special kenning
An expression spoken to refer
Suggest a similarity between
We call the best the cream
We, they, them, the metonymy
Choose a feature to explore
An attribute lost in war
Calm storm, invisible border, oxymoron
Joined together, true words or lie
Contradictory as the migrating herds
Let's make a person, a beautiful smile
Prosopopoeia, an abstract idea
A wish and hope to be free
Kick the bucket, doornail, daisies
Thirteen steps and then a rope
Legend, language, floating trope

IF NOT ME; WHO WOULD I BE

Seconds, minutes, hours, the date
Hands and a face, a little late
Splitting hairs, walk the line
Have no time, I'll share mine
Is it all planned or left to fate
Why this place, country or state
A path, a trail, follow the sign
Under the light of stars that shine
A sudden moment to anticipate
Study the odds, what's the rate
Plants, soil, taste fresh wine
Chosen food, time to dine
What is served, is on the plate
Mediocre, good, great, superb...
Lives of twists, turns, and rhyme
Find the highest mountain to climb
In my blood, hereditary trait
Years and years, a long, long wait...

THE LONG WALK

Peering into vast unlimited space
Closer and closer, still far away
Stepping, watching, feeling lonely
No path, just aimless choice
Rolling down a hill unknown
Pulling, repelling, a strong grip
Dare let go, release the fear
A place found, just the right fit
Instant, temporary, forever, never
Rebound once, twice, again...
Around n' round on the carrousel
Others there with me I see
Familiar faces, stare at me
Countryside, city, concrete, wood
Build a home on planet earth
Toss a stone, see water falling
Happiness with fortune wise
On display as all pass by
I turn my head, on my back I lie
Faces up and around the air
Please don't speak or say a word
Laughter and job well done...
Now champions, we have won
But I came only for the fun...

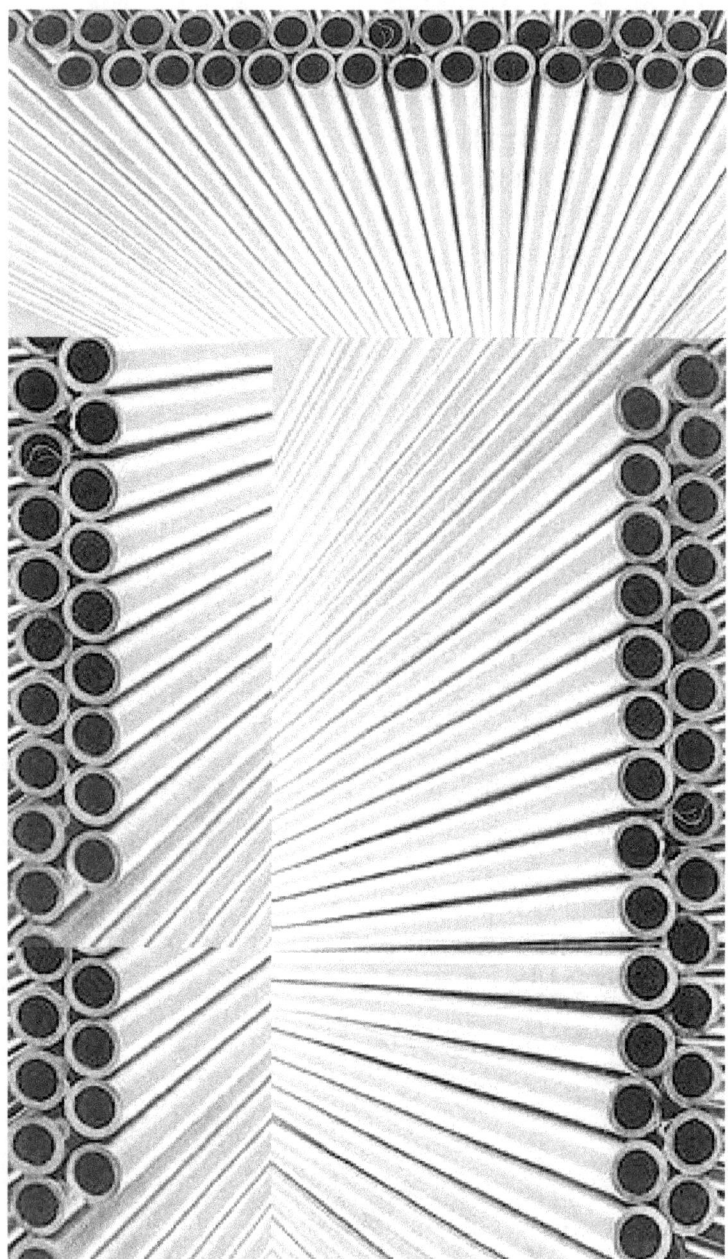

METAL ON METAL

Rolls of steel on rolls of steel connected with steel
Touching, scraping, grinding, sparks dropping, flying...
Beams of steel with ropes of steel carried upward...
Floating high above like feathers blowing in the wind
Bolted together with pins of steel, melting steel to fit
Living in steel, cold colorless metal dug from the earth
From bits and pieces made hard with fire and water
Working in steel day after day only to see the sun
From within riding on metal spinning tremendously
Sitting on steel to rest or sleep, falling skin on metal
Polished metal bent in directions with steel hammers
An audience, first prize for reflections in gleaming steel
Chains of steel to anchor ships of steel to carry steel
Loads of metal to make more steel chains of steel
Each link connected into a circle that has weight
No mortal man can hold while it continues to sink
Driving us mad with wonder as it rotates quickly
Pipes of steel twisted at unnatural angles and shapes
Delivering precious fluid for a sustainable complex life
Washing, cleaning, cutting, pulling, tools of steel
Hands from home, springs of steel, bodies of metal
Fingers, necks, gems with crowns of kings not found
Glass not to see, blades of iron, 1000-year history
Music of metal, iron horses around the golden sun
Imprinting man, industry, with numbers that abound...
Space and time alive and well, like all human kind...

ON FOOT

Forward one after another
Direction in the distance
Mountains I can see
Quickly resting under a tree

Looking down, legs, feet...
Steady, straight, strong, ambitious
Flesh and spirit, left and right
Colossal thinking above

Unselfish, noble, kindly deeds
Wanting dignity for all
Up in the world by each step
Found my hand too soft

Beyond callus and hard illusion
Wild adventures, free small world
Lined up next to each other
Youthful feeling of life, up-down

Enduring, resilient, granite stone
Melting holes in my sticky soles
Songs that are ringing merry
Into the bank of life, saved...

HITHER TO – HENCEFORTH

All that has been accomplished
From history knowledge filled
And the future it will become
Passed on from father to son
Stories then told to others
Trouble in paradise all around
Family above, below the ground
Keep the memory in the mind
Few with reaching power in hand
Control and fence the land
Entry or exit, this is the claim
Piece of paper, picture and name
Under the skin, a mark in sight
Groups meet in dead of night
People are friends, then disappear...
Stories and rumors we all hear
Last step taken without a fight
Darkness falling lost daylight...
A spirit of hope, grasp it tight
Ringing the air waves of sound
Strength of love, all or none
Passion for life, gift begun
On the path with you in kind
Judgment waiting, open arms
Untangle the back of your mind
Mercy please, time is done...

LIVING IN THE LIGHT

I read once and then I read twice
I read three times and once more
The last time I read I understood
Small, invisible, between the lines
A small detail can be missed
Even when known...
Some others do not see
In their haste it passed
Trying to see...
Looking at... air...
To the eye most hidden below...
A place where you may see...
What everyone is hoping to find
Even then it may not be seen
Open, direct, pointed out...
In view it sits waiting for you to take
The endless supply of knowledge
Waiting to be absorbed, an open door
Drink from the cup, lift the rock
Look under your feet, over your head
Dream from your pillow while in bed
Peel back the sky, discover beyond...
Stars above in view to reach...
No matter how high, listen the truth
Don't believe the lie, alone in the dark
Shine and sparkle...
Become a part of life that never dies...

LOVE TO TOUCH

Skin soft to touch...
Skin of color and size...
Breathing, growing, changing...
Delicate as a flower...
Tough oak... age by sight...
Bending in the wind...
Soaking up the light...
Drinking water to live... taking root...
Leaving home... scars of life...
Making me strong, friends and neighbors...
Blood kin... memories all wait within...
Floating away to a place...returning
again...looking different...change
feels the same...touch of love...
Wife, children, mother, sister, brother...
People I know...I say hello to the dog
in the street, fur soft...bird's wing...
The breeze...silk....fine...glass of wine...
Caress the face...touch the lace...
Leaves that glow...flowers bloom...
Spring...my wedding ring....musical
instrument that sings...wood, wire...
Brass...leather stretched over a barrel

Echoes of sound touch me...
Passing through an invisible spirit
honest and true, cold heat too...
Extreme...waking up after a kiss...
Was it a dream... birthday present
next to my bed...joyful child...big
oak tree with roots above ground
A place a free mind can see...
Climb to the top, hide between...
Round and round seasons change the
ground under my feet, in my toes...
fall on my nose, sunshine above
Things I love...touch...face...hand...
A book with words to tell me
how a person looks falling as
raindrops bounce up to the sky...
Sand in the desert, hot and dry
A wise man I met... up on a
mountain top...
Scrambling there to be alone...
Now wise mountain climbed...
The journey comes to an end...
Alone myself...love I leave...
life we weave... will touch...
Everyone we meet...

WINDOWS AND DOORS

Walking by windows
And... past doors
Everywhere I look
On roofs...on floors
Trains and planes
Have them too
Even the animals
At the zoo
Open or closed
Locked with a key
Hidden away
No one can see
Cobwebs hang down
Raindrops slide
Footsteps walk quickly
Safety behind
Knock...say hello
Smile...a greeting
Violins playing joyfully
I see life guarded
Some broken spirits
Nirvana the life
Open all windows and doors
you see closed...

QUAY

One afraid two fearless three weak four strong
Five happy six sad seven interested eight bored
Nine tired ten awake eleven poor twelve rich
Thirteen teach fourteen learn fifteen walk
Sixteen run seventeen sing eighteen talk
Nineteen work twenty play twenty-one win
Twenty-two lose twenty-three-laugh
Twenty-four cry twenty-five give twenty-six take
Twenty-seven sin twenty-eight forgive
Twenty- nine honest thirty lie thirty-one count
Thirty-two spell thirty-three buy thirty-four sell
HURRY...ME AND YOU...THERE'S A LOT TO DO
Thirty-five single thirty-six marry thirty-seven wake
Thirty-eight sleep thirty-nine lost forty found
Forty-one eat forty-two starve forty-three dream
Forty-four live forty-five listen forty-six see
Forty-seven remember forty-eight forget
Forty-nine appear fifty gone fifty-one a moment
One moment alive... one moment shine...
One moment bright... one moment change...
One moment repent... one moment gracious...
One moment new... one moment came...
One moment again... one moment done...
One moment at a time...thought in my mind...

CONSTITUTION

Paper with words and ink
Offering freedom, a way to think
Written by men and women
Endorsed, signed by elected people
Some who know of living life...
Put on display for all to see
Guarded by soldiers always...
Celebration, holiday every year
Power gathers at the base and top
In between people haven't a crop
Levi a tax on the work that's done
Distribute some, the rest gone
Let's all sing, we'll make up a song
A protest song to show what's wrong
Play it on the radio, CD, mp3
Paint a flag, fly it high above
News flash from the media spreads
Corruption, deception, spying...
Wealth, misfortune, sadness, crying...
Punishment, torture, mother-nature
One company, two or three, monopoly
No one to answer the telephone
Talking to a machine, I'm all alone
Inflation, expensive, save or buy
No place to park my car
Shopping mall, so many floors
Paper with words and ink
Offering freedom, a way to think

HOUSE OF THOUGHT

Through a window peering
Secrets invisible to all...
Known only to a few...
A lifetime of thought revealed
Told and shared, a gift to all
Observation-calculation-celebration

Many-many-counted years
Creating and spreading fears
Myth-legend-stories-fairy tales
Stars glowing on chosen places
Minds shift, questions answered
Expressions reflected on faces

Knowing what is in lieu waiting
Wisdom planted, growing now
Seeing and touching an idea
Persistent promise, held vow
Unrelentingly searched...sought
Shaking my mind, freeing thought...

SPAR WITH YOUTH

All points skyward, to every shore
Riding, floating, living on air
Keen sight, clear vision, speed
Strength, invincibility and courage
Tossing life without hesitation
Jumping, falling, rolling, laughing
Playing, walking, early and late
Ideas, creativity, wine and song
Mountains searched, found, climbed
Learn, experience, my memory
Experimentation, exploration, design
New for me and my friends too
Edge of a moment, reflection shine
Holding the tail for a short time
A beautiful face, just came along
Playtime begins and never ends...

SOME THINGS NEVER CHANGE

Early one mild, virgin morning
A benevolent declaration announced
Lampooning and revealing adage
Seasoned for the tranquil troupe

Some things never change
Cozy, snug, sheltered and secure
Antidote, cures, poison, perish
Longing intoxication, peaceful scorn

Scrub, scrub, polish and clean
Over and over, then one more time
Pain in the shoulder and hands
Asking for help along the way

Some things never change
Children laugh and shout
A skinned arm, leg or knee
Dog and cat in the yard

But those days have since gone
Pounding the pavement, interview
Application, this I should do
Do you have any questions?

Some things never change
Some people work for food
Others grind for some cash
Take, steal, sin, good and bad...

Honesty deep in the heart
Not a window to open and close
Known by all who you meet
In the end it will serve you well

A noble soul, old-fashion school
Trying to help, willing to defend
Not a thought to advance
A path, destiny or chance

Some things never change
Shadows from the sun
Stars and moon at night
Broken glass on the ground

Late one warm cultivated night
Watching the glow, reflecting...
Thoughts in mind, a song plays
Melody floats to my lips

Again and one more time
Fill the hours of the day
Animals singing their songs
Choking leash that's too tight

Tireless search, find a way
Open sky, birds on branches
A declaration and announcement
Bursting with energy to be free...

FOISTED - GALLERY

Recycled story, same old art
History hanging on a wall
Newspaper article, headline
Buy your tickets, buy your blues
No leader we want to follow
Kind, gentle, humble form
Chop down the trees, burn
Purpose lost, never found
Until buried deep underground
Breaking my knuckles

Eyes that see the purity
Young minds that imagine
No routine, but by chance
A line that turns endlessly
Crossing borders, free wake
Waves that engulf life
Air sweet with ideas
Never waver, always strong

PERIL

Down direct, high speed...
Pushing the peddles, more force
Quick glance, a look, a spot...
Heed the warning, all clear
Focus to the ramp and hill
Across to the other side
Time stops, dimensions collide
Through me the air did pass
Up the ramp I gloriously flew
Perfect jump and landing too
An angel watching over me
Young, foolish wild child
Not the first time...
Over and over, many times again
Desires also given, sometimes two
Watchful rescue from peril
Snatched for some reason
Hopefully fulfill this duty of mine
For this I will gladly spend my time...

SAINT REMY

A wall that surrounds
Exhausted come to rest
But there is no rest
Only a schedule to keep
Love breaks free from life
Becomes unrelenting passion
Day and night...twists...turns
Visions suspended in air
Change what's seen by all
To an image in mind
Slice of a moment in time
...Painted on canvas
...Hung on a wall
Colors flowing in a frame...

INERTIA

Throughout our body it flows
Pressure, gravity and hope
Forward, up, round...down
Small universal living body
Following light, losing night
Traveling long distance far
Returning again, changing site
Perpetual, liberating adventure
Energy, mass, total control
In concert, keeping time
Asleep, awake, stop and roll
Heartbeat, pumping love...
A living, growing vine...
Weight of the dimensional world
Floating through a narrow window
Threads of life...cosmic life...

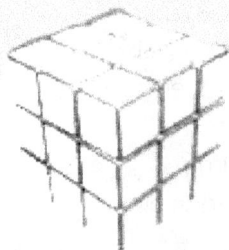

ABC

011235813...

ELEMENT

A point line or a plane
Member of a group, grain
Pieces, sets, connected shine
Unseen by the naked eye

Essential, irreducible, fundamental
Principles, assumptions of what is...
Entity, geometric size, shape
With the trees and apes

Generations, configuration, angles
This treat seen, now untangle...
Determinant array-constitute matrix
Universal substance into the mix

Identical, normal, pleasant atoms
Earth, wind, air, and fire
Strings and holes, electric wire
Temperature change, pounding drum

Forces over and beyond control
Severe, distinct, his and her
Ultimate, ancient ingredient
Alphabet, spinning down a hole...

OLE

Count the innumerable years
Moving forward... always slowly
Looking back, time, stage, history
Vantage point this parallax
From there... witness time...

Past links, gloriously simple...
Known by many...
Written down...recorded
Important for time to ring
Start and finish by the bell

Run, roll, fall, winner declared
Sitting next to the old world
Rest for a time, relax, enjoy...
Burst forth into a rainbow....
Paint it across the sky....

Edges glowing with energy
Touching the ends unseen
This is only in our dreams
Read about on paper, in books
A reflection slowly changing

Rotating, warping, bending
Going I know... but where...
Leaving the world behind
Tomorrow, future unsure
Now my choice has creed

Wait, go back, step forward
All will change this moment
Decision, choice and faith
There all around I see
A step taken to be free...

PANNIERS

Pockets full...no space, no place
Thoughts of how to carry the load
A necessity of modern life
How was it done long ago?
On someone's back, bag, sack
Animal's burden stepping slow
On shoulders, held with hands
Lightweight, weaved together
Over and under held strong
All shapes and size...the prize
Carried over distance long
Precious load, container made
Used many times and again
Stones to build on... break
Under the cover lives a snake
Skill and knowledge of will
Medicine, food and clothes
Reeds of mesh protect
Under a tree they are sold
Passing by, reflection in my eye
This is the spot, the place
Weaving life, step by step
Carried and held with grace
At home a freshly caught meal
Kept, held, softly in my creel

HERBAGE

Thick growth beyond view
Smoke-filled air and room
Clouds of night, hand above
Touching life and in control
Engineer, build, produce, use
No connection, invisible wire
Floating on soft green grass
Above an open, clear blue sky
Dreams, thought in my mind
Pieces of the puzzle are placed
A picture now becomes clear
Age has given me sight
Value beyond any price
Fear lost, instinct remains
Around it grows, tall, strong,wide
Protection, safety, a sweet home
Surrounded by family never alone...

TESTER

Looking serious...looking tough...
Judging how we move and act
Learning lessons, sitting still
In a chair, behind a desk
Clock ticking away slowly
Girl in front and on either side
What am I learning today?
Numbers hard to calculate
Speeches I don't understand
Walls all around... growing tall
Bells ring, quickly out the door
Nothing to carry... all left behind
Lying on a bed, dream in my mind
Shapes spinning, sliding ground
Sleep silent without sound
The game-travel east or west
Up in the morning, late at night
Twenty four hours ticking away
Now we are done for the day
Second chance, try once more...
Living life...battle and war...

KARAT 24 PURE

Dug from this sphere so round
Toiling until time now gone
Ringing melody of hammers sound
Sleep can't escape, dream in song
Silent, tied and bound...
Voices beckon, to come along
Twisted tight, completely wound
Confused between right and wrong
Now and then, feel the prong
In my mind, thoughts abound
Lyric-melody, with a tune to bond
Life since gone, begins to hound
It springs from nature's ground
Growth is new, quiet and strong
Treasure we see all around
Can this be where I belong?
What I've searched... finally found

MOMENT WITHIN

Uncovered from hidden fold
Dream once thought lost
Slight moment-today we hold
Caught-frozen in dissolving frost
Deep sleep released in dreams
Forgotten detail muse remains
Images not what they seem
Straight at me-changing lanes
Moments collapse before an end
Static panorama-motile closer still
Absorbed as it begins to bend
This new world comes to occupy
Swarming up around my legs
Melting-framing colors brilliant
More time the old world begs
Strong resistance-a futile fight
Crowning-watch helplessly
One last glance to look around
Closing my eyes-one last chance
Nothing left but the sound
At last the final note quietly fades
Let go the group-soon the touch
Approaching shadow-cool shade
Free time-tired old clutch
Kiss goodbye- lips that touch

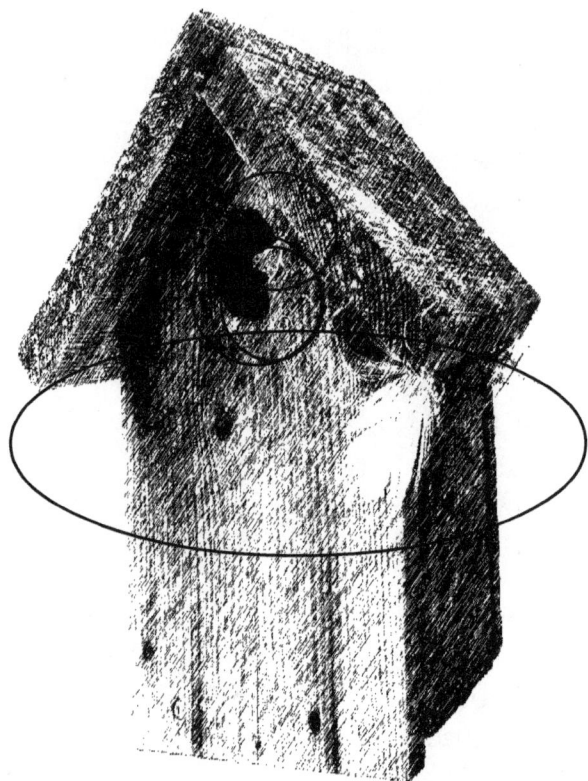

BIRD HOUSE

Weathered wood about to break
Long ago made by human hand
Everywhere kept in the trees
To the tune in the morning I wake
Over to a window, stand and gaze
Glorious cries, sounds to be free
A thin branch begins to shake
My last thought falling fast
Rolling to a stop, resting there
Around me canvas growing vast
Through wind and rain I am lost
The bite of cold, falling snow
Ice melting drops, thunder very slow
Southern sun helps the grass grow
From the earth and all around
There I lay waiting to be found
Suddenly a pentatonic sound
Searching food from the ground
Thinking only, get back to the tree
There is no way, impossibility
Not a natural nest for them to be...
Old broken wood, paint and memory
Falling to the ground, changed forever
This was once a resting place
Disappearing without a single trace

THE CURATOR

Under the watchful eye
Never a moment alone
Through the hills and rooms
Carefully checking the prize

Dust collecting in the corner
Floating in rays of sunlight
That pierce the wall
A vast umbra of space

Hollow walls, bottomless pit
Stairway leads to a stairway
Routine and blank thoughts
Until the treasure seen

This moment, uncounted time
Precious picture of reflection
Expand outward on mountains
A single flash of life

Threading the needle of success
A tailor-made jewel
Priceless, valuable, cruel
Senses tell me what to do

I lift and place my hand
Unknowing, hapless, lost fool
Echoing voices follow me
As a shadow watches from above

Never ending season of rain
Long hard sledge hammer
Kept next to a burning flame
Looking for the stolen scream

SCALE

What is given weight today?
Decide/think/contemplate
The bending branch/anticipate

What and who will rise then fall
Resistance/balance/a brick wall
Avoirdupois/support/very tall

Incomplete time will hover/fate
When you arrive early/late
Mind of knowledge love/hate

Changing shape/lifetime growth
On my hand/choose another
Just one/opposite or both

List before we concentrate
Attraction/repel/powerful force
Gravity action/where's the source

Whose idea was it to weigh
Sun and moon/night and day
Black and white/shades of gray

Everyday on my body claws
Spin/stumble/stand/fall
When will it stop/wind up again

Reverse the forward hand of time
Is it possible to break the law?
Fear falling into the maw

Thoughts melt on sunshine
Connecting dots with rhyme
With the sun/past and prime

How much does time weigh?
Countless/endless line of gray
I have to go/I want to stay

FOLLY

Running to catch a train
Umbrella closed in the rain
Playing and winning at solitaire
Thinking about what clothes to wear
Shopping, buying things of no need
Pruning and cutting the simple weed
Seconds and thirds off the plate
Fishing without any kind of bait
Watching TV to enrich my mind
Back to zero after number nine
Figure out a magician's trick
Looking at the hands of time
Burning the candle wick
Holding my breath to exercise
Buying on credit and later pay
Looking for buried treasure
This is real, continually told
Unread books on a library shelf
Fountain of youth, live a long time
Linking human kind to oozing slime
Suddenly regret, take another footstep
Here comes another sudden regret
Dream or thought, in a trap caught
Beaten and bloody, the battle fought

WALKING ON BARS OF LIGHT

There they are for me to see
Glowing effervescent in the night
Powerful for thought and life
Below, above, all sides, beyond
Going up, down, and all around
A straight line, turning sharp
Taut and tight, then a pair
More lines and the sum agree
Everywhere surrounded, all of me
Glowing and dimming as I stare
In my mind, controlling light
Wands, bars rolling over themselves
Rushing on and to the shore
Taking my memories far away
An empty shell, an open space
Sparkling in my eyes brightly
The mirror of life
Reflecting, glimmering, piercing
Infinite threads of white
Angels and stars of night

LUCRE

Earn, pay, a gift, income
Bank account in my name
Skill, ability, for sale, bid
Borrow and lend, foreclose, call
The game of money, win and lose
The house rests, spit and chew
Retirement comes anonymously
Sell the treasure, buy all new
Show me some card, then describe
Is this a joke, what should I do?
My right, but then you decide
Your fight, go along for the ride
We pay cash and a bonus as well
How much value is put on time?
Who decides legality or crime?
Ownership of material and goods
Lease or rent some space
Investment for the future race
Images stare directly at you
Holding ideas, the sky is blue
Let's talk it over, barter and trade
Numismatist, coin is my life
Waiting there behind showroom glass
In sight, far from in hand
Impossible to reach from where I stand

FRENZY

Hair standing on end
Perspiration rolling down a brow
Tingling energy, fingertips and toes
A face sees a face turn away
Moving quickly in one place
There must be a way up...
A charge by all, across the street
Shopping spree, on sale today
A parking space not to be found
Up to the top and back down
Searching pockets for coins
Driving across railroad tracks
Flashing red lights in the mirror
For a moment, hold my breath
Smoke and fire, incinerate
Locked inside and no escape
What will happen, anticipate
Air and all what's left, taken away
Fall to the floor, choking core
Forgotten time, end is near
Upside down, twisted around
Then a voice heard, again, again...
Saved by the heroic unselfish brave
For me their life they gave
No reward or Medal of Honor
Great deed at the moment of truth

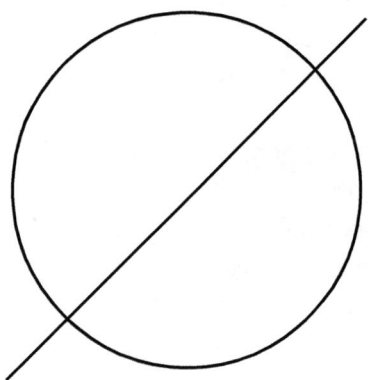

AXIS

The line that no one sees
An angle vertical, a deep freeze
Slowly melting changing form
Climate continuing to warm
In places cutting down trees
Hard rains and powerful storm
Scientists test, research concludes
We're using too much black crude
Success, status, measured, sued
Books are written, read, believed
The author tells a story weaved
Propaganda fills...floats the wind
Flowers painted on the wall
Incurvity, a circle, a vertical pin
24/7 seven around the clock
Progenitor, a key to unlock

ELEVATOR

Round the corner, stand waiting momentarily
Looking at a watch, looking in a shoulder bag
Short conversation on a cell phone
Wait is over, doors open simultaneously
Welcome passengers with a cheer
Step aboard, no reason to fear
People scurry into the miniature box
Eyes spike to the numbers above
Last chance to flee for safety
Closing doors, blinking lights
Cables pull, rolling smoothly
Sudden stop, clunk, the next level, stop again
Some get off, just three left in...
Only one button left, light lit at the top
Just then we stop...
Let's not panic, just keep cool
Push a button, call on the emergency phone
Uncountable minutes, priceless time
Lights go out, no window, no sunshine
Fifteen hours we are all alone
Eyes always meet, fragrance, old shoe
Sound of echoes, slice the air
A dimly lit ceiling is the only other view
The box begins to move upward
Destiny in sight, we stop again, doors open...
We're greeted by people unknown to us
I've since forgotten why I'm here...
To be free...?

BLINK

In the blink of an eye
The tear that falls
Has a love that holds on tight
In the blink of an eye
The smile I see
Has joy that fills an empty heart
In the blink of an eye
The hardest thing I ever said
Was goodbye
No matter how far or how long
We are apart
We stand together
You're forever in my heart

BOND OF LOVE

Bond of love - Unbroken chain
Never apart - Will always remain

Bond of love - Memory to keep
In my thoughts - At night I sleep

Bond of love - Today and beyond
A wish come true - Coin tossed in a pond

Bond of love - Meant to be free
Mind and soul - Two hearts agree

Bond of love - In my arms
Together and close - Safe from what harms

Bond of love - Your hand in mine
This warm touch - Under stars that shine

Bond of love – Footsteps on the ground
A trail of our life – Love is found

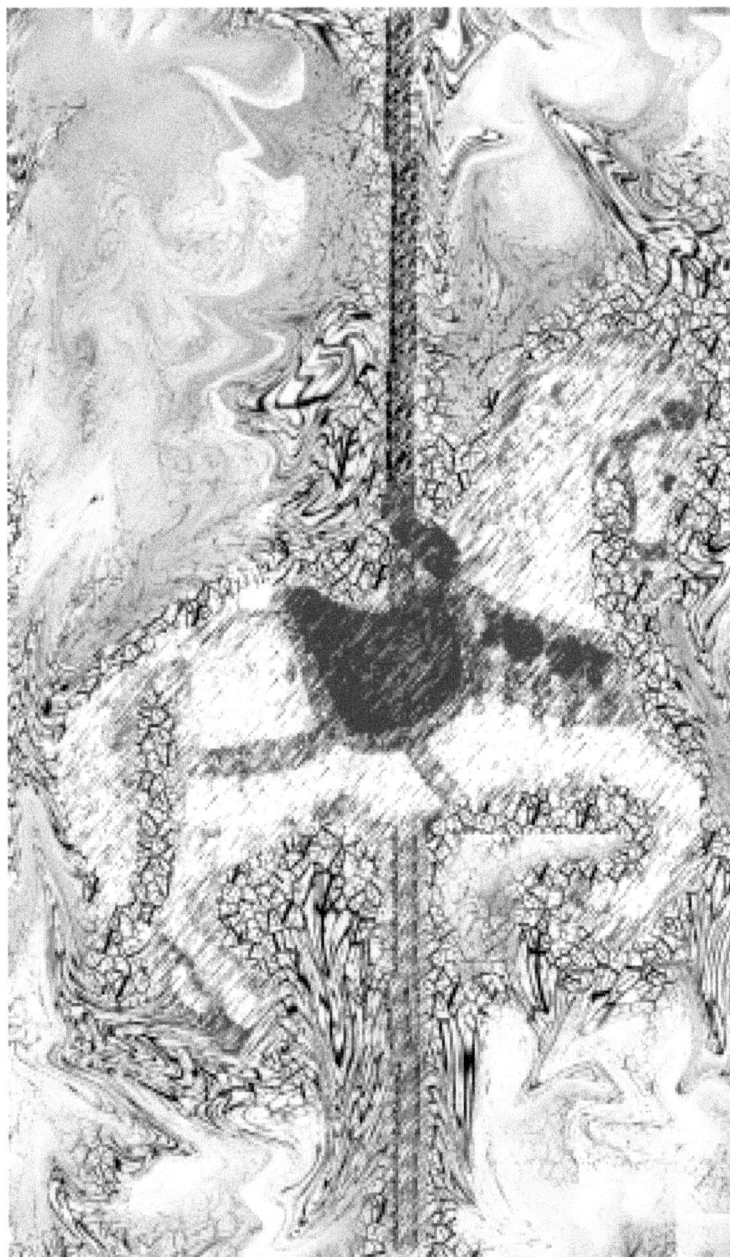

GET OUT OF YOUR HEAD

Get out of your head
Fly somewhere else instead
Get out of your head
See yourself – See yourself

Before you run out of time...

Learn how to play the game
Learn how to live the game
Learn how to play the game
Be yourself – Be yourself

Before you run out of time...

There's a trap set for you
Everyone's caught except a few
There's a trap set for you
Free yourself – Free yourself

Before you run out of time...

Step on this lonely planet
First watch and follow
Step on this lonely planet
Teach yourself – Teach yourself

Before you run out of time...

MOON AND SUN

Tell me, what is the moon?
How many stars are above?
Limitless forever, lunch at noon
White-winged floating dove
Spreading a message, peace, love
Hanging midnight, big white balloon
I love it, fits just like a glove
Children grow up way too soon
Out of my way, push and shove
Alone in paradise, flowing sand dune
Standing in the middle, watch it revolve
Vanishing, melting, shadows bloom
There is only one that can...
 See /smell / touch / hear / feel /
What turns the mysterious wheel...

NORMAL

Feet on the ground firm
Following a path leading somewhere
To go seems the logical decision
Second thoughts enter my mind
Stopping to think of what will be
The choices slap me in the face
Wake up, look up, see, embrace...
Hold to life, grip it tight
Narrow mind, someone blind
From all points shone the light
See it glow from one's face
Round and round the ground no trace
Falling from the sky, open arms
Washing, cleansing, flowing, bending...
Faster and faster down and locked
Deepest well, sound the alarm
Another soul saved from harm...

MAUGRE

The price is high but perhaps I pay
No light to see what I read
Remember me, I'll remember you
Crawl and scratch my way out
Strong heart but feeble old body
The scars are there to see
Plot thickens, watch dice roll
Moment of time becomes short
Sudden scurry to learn the moves
Turn toward the sun for light
Look for water down below
One barrier after another
Something above or a step below
Change inside, nurture and grow
Always another rock, stepping stone
Music of life, sounds that drone
Slap in the face, harvest moon

HORIZON

Horizontal circular smooth line
Earth-sky...seen...above-below
Continually-constantly-connected
Trees spring from the surface
Clouds float from the sky
Every direction, living perfection
Winds touch waves moving free
Light sprinkles and dances
Rain falls, nourishment from high
Star light, moon light, bright white
From high-direction to view
The point seen by everyone
Impossible site to obscure
Ever changing moment in time
Always different-never the same
Description-simple word-beautiful

BILLETDOUX

Standing there for the first time
Beauty, youth, eyes that care
Vibrant emotion, heart-beat climb
Fire on the wind, together we soar
Above mountains, higher than clouds
Out and away from the crowds
Sweeping the shore to the sea
Unforgettable memories stay
Smile, expression of joy
Word, song, special melody
Hands of love gently caress
Resting on pillows, soft as clouds
My arm covers my brow
Grasp one last brilliant moment
Hope that image will come true
But this is just the dream of a boy

MAD MAN

Two steps, side step, then run
A rocket shot out of a cannon
Moving, never standing still
Physical body, mind and will
Holding on to a rope for life
Being dragged through, across
Picked up, thrown down hard
Pushed against the wall, fence
With all breath, harness a scream
Indulgence, experiment, dream
Bury the needle, the top speed
Sound barrier, life abounds
Thunder and lighting storm
Closer and closer to the edge
One more time, the same way
Flocks of birds in the sky
The brick wall once more
Into pieces the image destroy

Before

Then---Now

After

SKIEN

Complexity, mystery, clues untangle
Odd, even, primary or composite
The story of life is so told
Long coils of years and history
Threads connected by names, places
Carried on by the family line
Born under similar glowing stars
Distinguished, wealthy and powerful
Controlling all of man's priceless time
Secret meetings on distant pomona
Fibre made, affixed to the skein
The adder coils around life...
Jocose the oafish and mendicant
Their disciples puff and expand
Offering treasure to the diadems
The lichen grows ubiquitously fast
A sublime echo floats through...by...
Paradise and immortality awaits
Socrates, Aristotle, Xanthous
Then an empty skein rolls absent
An end is reached, the line gone
Unraveled life, sound in history
Old flag taken down, new one raised
Currency borrowed on one's life
Unknowingly agreed to this debt
As time ticks, we earn and defray

AKIMBO

Listen to the beat...
Hear it...
Bump/bump/bump/ba/ba/bump...
Bump/bump/bump/ba/ba/bump...
Bump/bump/bump/ba/ba/bump...
Tap your foot, count, count...
Standing tall, hands on hips
All together now...one more time
Elbows out, back and forth...
Do you know or remember?
A song you've heard or sung
Whistle a tune, howl at the moon
Around the fire dance and shout
Into the glowing sky, go flames go...
Under foot the beat remains...
A pose now and long ago...
Akimbo...
Bump/bump/bump/ba/ba/bump...
Bump/bump/bump/ba/ba/bump...
Bump/bump/bump/ba/ba/bump...

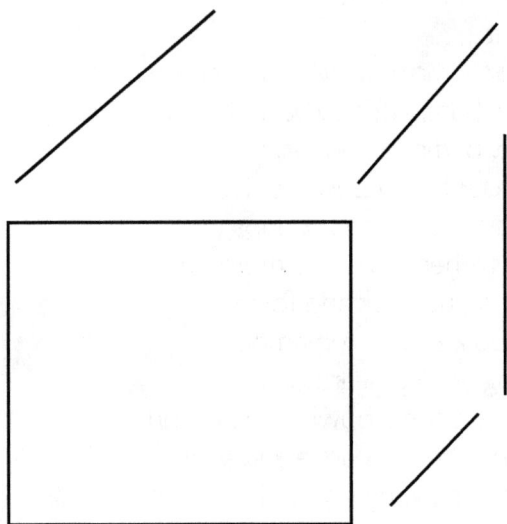

CORNFLAKES

The box is full...
The box is closed...
The box is open...
The box is empty...

MORPHISM

One to one or between
A reaction, wipe the slate clean
An image and reflection seen
Composition made from memory
Back to back, shake a hand
Head resting on my shoulder
Breakfast with coffee and cream
Can't remember, nightmare or dream
On a pole, around and around
Who sees who, while we turn?
A thought goes up to open skies
Teardrops fall from sad eyes
Footsteps, fingertips, clues...
Blind following the fool
Touch everyone with my thought
Ideas are stretched beyond sight
There is no image in front of me
From the beginning, then start
Imagine, conceive, formulate
Smoke will rise or fall
Love accepted, hate denied
The universe is a distant outsider...
That is where the soul resides...

SLED

Out the frost-covered window
I gaze with happy delight
On the hill across the road
Covered in a blanket of snow
My friends making their way up
Behind them dragging and pulling
The essence of winter speed
Short, long, new and old
Metal, wood, kids, fearless, bold
To the top they trudge along
No longer can I sit and watch
Knowing where I want to be
My face pressed against the glass
Flying down the hill so carefree
Out the door to make it true

Sighted in our garage above
Twisting and carefully removing
Until it falls gently into my arms
Out to the mountains I climb
Down friends fly barking
Soon my turn will arrive
At the crest I stand breathless
Quick run, then belly flop
Sailing the white powder alive
Still the feeling I remember
Many years after, still strong
Those days in the afternoon
A winter once in a blue moon
One long day, over too soon...

ELEGANT MAN

Never tiring of this daily activity
Refreshing site for sore eyes
Conspicuous, ubiquitous, revealing
Sunny bright, moon star bright
Ups and downs, side by side
Fingers, forks, knives, and spoons
Simple, plain, common, elegant man
Cold, warm, hot, moist, wet, dry
No longer a hunter by day or night
Burning wood, open-fire cooking
Follow step by step this recipe
Microwave, refrigerate, toast, blend
Organic, chemical, pesticide, suicide
Survival, my daily activity gone
Temporary place, visiting guest
Search for what is kind, gentle, fine
Building bridges to narrow minds
Living from and off the land
Mixture, pattern, height, wits
Do what you can, elegant man...

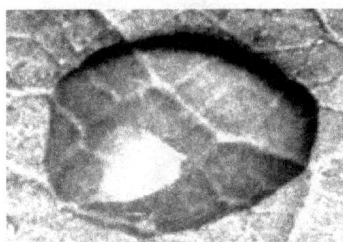

DROP OF DEW

Born with desire and instinct
Flirtation, touch, gentle caress
Dalliance, frivolous dawdling
Spending time on needless desire
Lacking interest, surmounting boredom
All moments alive with curiosity
Parallel ideas, opposite directions
Seen in the morning, late evening
Glowing, shining, glistening bright
Miniature world, delicate state
My eye revolves, observing beauty
Enjoyment in :countless:timeless:space:
Then it floats and rises high above
Soon gone without a single trace
Melting into mist, becoming air...
Touching all with one breath
Splendor spread by all life
The circle begins and ends
Repetition, cycle up and down
One tiny world disappears...

REWARD

Dynamite idea, fortune bequeath
Gold medal, some cash too
The winner, a prize granted
Where to sign up, stand in line
Recommendation from people
Men and women have a notion
Give the unknown poet his due
Professional cliché, shall we choose
Trophy for the best show
Plated in gold, head to toe
Accolades, money, for your part
If offered, would you perform?
Starve-soul...muscle...mind...
Pay for existence to find...
See more than others do
Colors of variety, old and new
Impressions, patterns, design
Appearing out of the blue
Glittering on a gown wide
Up steps of a mountain side
Hidden in the gin of wood
Embedded life, frozen eternity
They discuss, reward, and decide
Who will be the lucky one?
All, hope, want, wish, pay
Dan David, make my day

YOU ARE HERE

O

BLIND ZONE

Invisible to the eye, all around
Nano zone of complex structures
From them ideas now abound
The spyglass breaks the code
Our world, we place the fixtures
At that time, we all see
Discovery and useful purpose
Flowing river along the road
It grows and lives among us
Gain skill, ability, instinct...
Future world inside, doorway out
Book covers, a picture, words...
A pin hole contains the cosmos

January	February	March

April	May	June

July	August	September

October	November	December

YESTERDAY-TOMORROW

Open the paddock, let me run
Show me the tricks of the trade
I'm fresh, young, strong and willing
Making lines, connecting dots
Dreams filling raw empty spaces
Burning unharnessed, rising flame
Knocking randomly on doors, walls
Freedom waiting on the other side
New space, new hindrance, waiting
Always another barrier or puzzle
With spring love begins to call
Calculations, courtship, celebrations
Geometric shapes, contracts, dates
Meet the deadline, run out of time
Stopped dead in my tracks
Pushed down and buried deep
No escape this cell I sleep
Then one day the gifts arrive
Universal in manner they count
From then on I never doubt
I give thanks in many ways
For one new tomorrow...
And all my yesterdays...

X

YUD

Metric system
Ten
The doge
Ten
Great council
Ten
Fingers and toes
Ten
The Shofar blast
Ten
Generations from Adam to Noah
Ten
Kings to rule the world
Ten
Commandments
Ten
Plagues for Pharaoh
Ten
Wheel of fortune - forbbiden magic
Ten
Grams of tea leaves
Ten
Minyan
Ten
The holy nature of reality
Ten
Life, death, beginning, end!
X

Books by John Siwicki

Poetry

Inflexation
Fences
The Poetry of Food and Drink
Are You Casablanca

Novels

ExPRESSION

www.slabypress.com

www.ingramcontent.com/pod-product-compliance
Lightning Source LLC
Chambersburg PA
CBHW061751020426
42331CB00006B/1424